The Emma Press Anthology of Aunts

OTHER TITLES FROM THE EMMA PRESS

POETRY ANTHOLOGIES

Urban Myths and Legends: Poems about Transformations
The Emma Press Anthology of the Sea
This Is Not Your Final Form: Poems about Birmingham

POETRY BOOKS FOR CHILDREN

Falling Out of the Sky: Poems about Myths and Monsters
Watcher of the Skies: Poems about Space and Aliens
Moon Juice, by Kate Wakeling
The Noisy Classroom, by Ieva Flamingo

PROSE PAMPHLETS

Postcard Stories, by Jan Carson
First fox, by Leanne Radojkovich
Me and My Camera, by Malachi O'Doherty (Nov '17)
The Secret Box, by Daina Tabūna (Nov '17)

POETRY PAMPHLETS

Dragonish, by Emma Simon
Pisanki, by Zosia Kuczyńska
Who Seemed Alive & Altogether Real, by Padraig Regan
Paisley, by Rakhshan Rizwan

THE EMMA PRESS PICKS

Malkin, by Camille Ralphs
DISSOLVE to: L.A., by James Trevelyan
The Dragon and The Bomb, by Andrew Wynn Owen
Meat Songs, by Jack Nicholls
Bezdelki, by Carol Rumens

THE EMMA PRESS
Anthology of Aunts

Edited by Rachel Piercey and Emma Wright

With poems by Natalya Anderson, J V Birch,
Lily Blacksell, Stephen Bone, Carole Bromley,
Kayo Chingonyi, Mary Anne Clark, Tracy Davidson,
Brian Docherty, Charlotte Eichler, Amy Evans,
Matthew Haigh, Robert Hamberger, Jan Heritage,
Hilaire, Kathleen Jones, Angela Kirby, Gill Learner,
Rachel Long, Gill McEvoy, David McKelvie, Mia,
Joan Michelson, Isabel S. Miles, Winifred Mok,
Margot Myers, Anita S. Pulier, Kim M. Russell,
Elisabeth Sennitt Clough, Ruthie Starling, Rob Walton,
Kate White, Simon Williams and Anna Woodford

Illustrated by Emma Wright

THE EMMA PRESS

For our aunts

☙

THE EMMA PRESS

First published in Great Britain in 2017 by the Emma Press Ltd

Poems copyright © individual copyright holders 2017
Selection copyright © Rachel Piercey and Emma Wright 2017
Introduction copyright © Rachel Piercey 2017
Illustrations copyright © Emma Wright 2017

All rights reserved.

The right of Rachel Piercey and Emma Wright to be identified as the editors of this work has been asserted by them in accordance with the Copyright, Designs and Patents Act 1988.

ISBN 978-1-910139-66-0

A CIP catalogue record of this book
is available from the British Library.

Printed and bound in Great Britain
by TJ International, Padstow.

The Emma Press
theemmapress.com
queries@theemmapress.com
Birmingham, UK

Contents

Introduction, by Rachel Piercey vii

Travelling with Isaac, by Anna Woodford 1
The things they wrote, by Rob Walton 2
Sudbury Lunch, by Natalya Anderson 3
The Butcher's Diamond, by Anita S. Pulier 4

A Cuddle of Aunts, by Winifred Mok 7
Great-Aunt Rose, by Gill McEvoy 9
Curfew, by Kayo Chingonyi 10
A Half-Cut Sestina, by David McKelvie 11
Betsey Trotwood sets the record straight, by Carole Bromley 12

Aunt Amy's Parasol, by Angela Kirby 14
Auntie Peg, by Isabel S. Miles 15
Tailors, by Simon Williams 17
Jon Snow and the Joyces, by Jan Heritage 18
Aunt Syl, by Joan Michelson 20
She tells her nephew he's mad to get more tats, by Kate White ... 21
My Favourite Aunt, by Brian Docherty 22
The Sex Lives of Aunts, by Margot Myers 24
Coal Tar, by Stephen Bone 26

Survivors, by Charlotte Eichler 28
What Will Your Sims Do Now? by Matthew Haigh 29
Broken Biscuits, by Kathleen Jones 30

Aunty, by Rachel Long	32
Elizabeth Garrett Anderson Wing, by Mia	35
For the Aunts of Eighties Metal, by Elisabeth Sennitt Clough	37
Auntie Australia, by J V Birch	38
My oddest aunt, by Gill McEvoy	39
Sister, by Amy Evans	40
Holiday in Clacton, by Kim M. Russell	43
My Colourful Aunt Rose, by Tracy Davidson	44
The Alphabet Aunties, by Ruthie Starling	45
Familiar, by Mary Anne Clark	47
From the Duck-Egg Blue Kitchen, by Lily Blacksell	48
Auntie Bob's Feet, by Gill Learner	50
I sometimes hear her voice brekking, by Rob Walton	51
On becoming an aunt, by Hilaire	52
Aunt Anna, by Robert Hamberger	53
Acknowledgements	55
About the poets	56
About the editors	62
About the Emma Press	63
Also from the Emma Press	64

Introduction

"Now that you are become an Aunt, you are a person of some consequence & must excite great Interest whatever You do. I have always maintained the importance of Aunts as much as possible…" So wrote Jane Austen in 1815, to her ten-year-old niece Caroline. Anyone familiar with Austen's work will know that this is true: her aunts – Anne Elliot, Lady Catherine, Miss Bates, Mrs Gardiner et al – stride fully-formed around the centre of her plots, laughing, scolding, counselling and caring.

I am blessed in having an abundance of Mrs Gardiners in my life: fun, loving, supportive aunts whom I adore. This anthology is for them – I know that the trail-blazing, advice-giving, feast-cooking, fast-chatting, music-loving, gift-giving, high-kicking aunts collected here will make them smile.

The book also celebrates the lovely phenomenon of the unrelated 'aunt', the close family friend. 'Aunt' isn't simply a word describing a biological relationship; we use it to signify closeness, connection and a nurturing presence – as well as the agony aunt's ability to give smart and objective advice. There are many such inspiring, influential figures here.

But there are cloudier stories, too – aunts who have been trapped by the times, by bad luck, by their socioeconomic circumstances. And so the anthology also functions as an important historical account of women's experiences: alongside the exuberantly convention-busting aunts, we encounter those who lost their only loves to war, who never had the children or the lives they longed for, who have been misunderstood or neglected by impatient younger relatives.

Whatever the situation, each poem offers a hugely memorable encounter. I loved this submission process – it was wonderful to meet such bold, formidable, heartbreaking, hilarious individuals and I treasure every aunt in this anthology. Reader, I am delighted to introduce you to so many persons of consequence.

Rachel Piercey
LONDON
April 2017

The Emma Press Anthology of Aunts

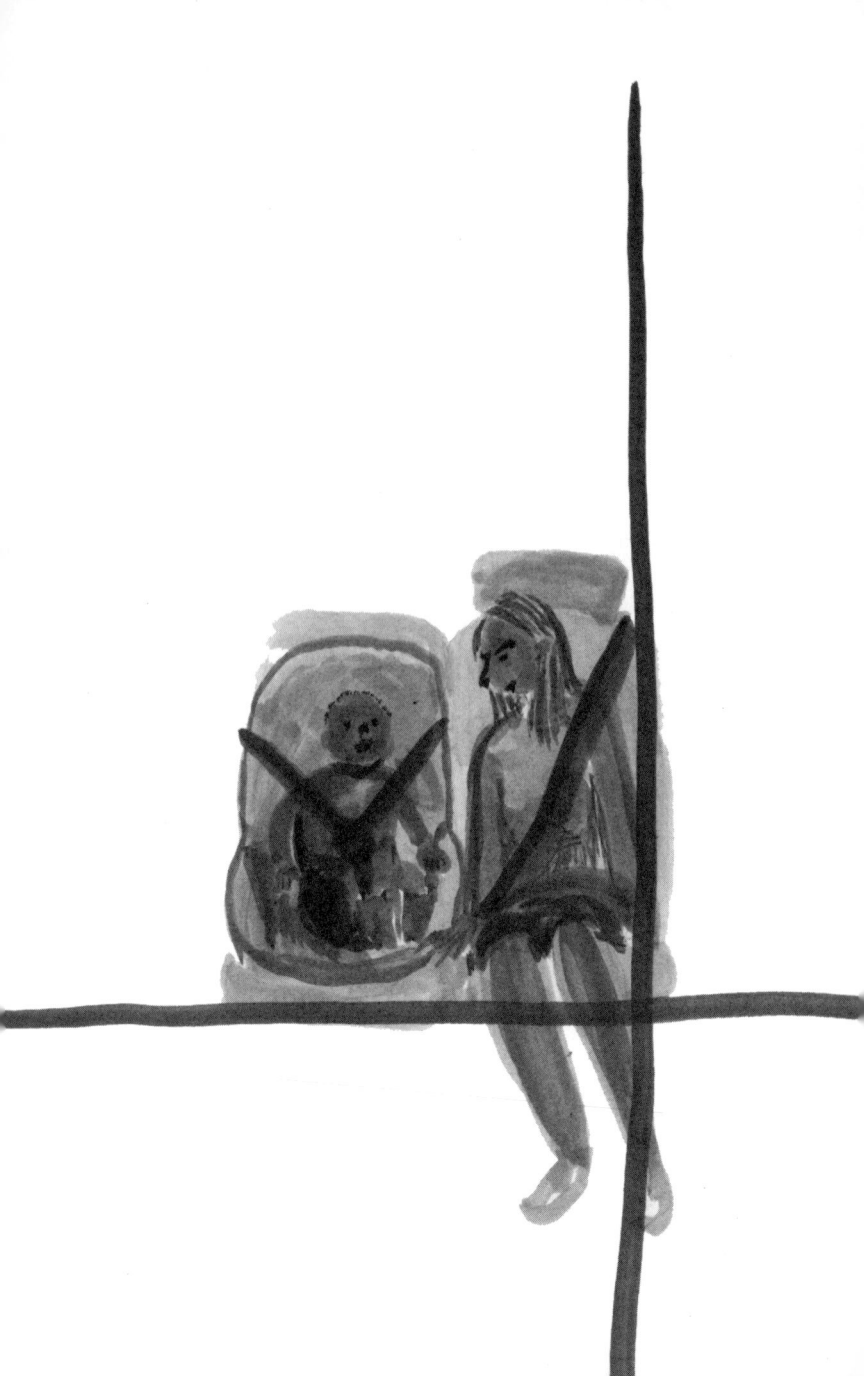

ANNA WOODFORD

Travelling with Isaac

Tired of toys, you play
with your voice –
'A-ba!' 'Ah-ba!'

I find a couple of words
for you to chew on like 'apple'
and 'auntie' but *'A-ba!'* you insist.

Then I begin to follow –
'A-ba!' I reply.
Suddenly we are speaking

to each other and
holding each other
in and outside of conversation

while, outside the car window,
moo-cows and choo-choos gather.
I want the car to go on for ever.

'How long
before they start to know
what they are saying?' I find myself

saying to your father, and he laughs
and tunes me out with the radio – 'Who knows,
Yada! Yada!'

ROB WALTON

The things they wrote

They wrote birthday cards
and *pound of pork sausages (not beef!)*,
lists of clothes: *sandals, cagoules, cardigans*
to take on coaches bound for Skegness
or Blackpool or Filey.
Once a well-known resort
in Spain: *sun cream.*
They wrote orders
for Avon catalogues
and Christmas hamper schemes.
They wrote when you went to the chip shop
with *+ scraps* underlined twice.
If you were out, they wrote notes:
Love Aunty, Love Auntie, Love Aunt.

NATALYA ANDERSON

Sudbury Lunch

Corners creased, it depicts our summer
visits at their best: Grandma launching
towards Auntie with a wooden spoon;
Auntie on her knees, arms on the counter,
throwing her head back. If Grandma gained
a lot of weight, or if Auntie lost it, the women
could pass as twins. Their hair – dark brown,
set. Cheeks slick, deep rose. In the background
a beefy bum peeking out from tinfoil, steam
caught mid-release from speckled roasting
pan. I look closer, can almost hear the men
on the balcony with their smokes. 'Why
can't they just do ham sandwiches, for Chrissake?'

The Butcher's Diamond

Aunt Freda got the diamond from her lover,
the butcher who refused to marry her
because his wife was in an institution.

After many ruinous years
she left him and gave the diamond
to my mother Ida.

Gentle Ida, who at twenty
fell in love with Freda's brother
after seeing him raise a clenched fist
from a soapbox at Brooklyn college,

reciting Marxist dicta against
the unequal distribution of wealth.
Ida, a shopkeeper's daughter,
unfamiliar with jewels,

liberated the little diamond
from its ringed prison to
a thin gold necklace
looped around her neck.

At her death, I unclasped the lock,
slid it off and held it
in my clenched fist.

It had so little to recommend it,
the butcher's diamond.
And I believe

it carries Freda's disappointment
and Ida's ambivalence.
Yet, I choose to wear it daily,

as even with its flaws
it sparkles when the light is right.

WINIFRED MOK

A Cuddle of Aunts

On grandma's birthday my aunts gather.
Flown in across continents, they feast
like bears on the love of their children,
grandchildren, hungry for smiles, cuddles,
time. Four mothers, four hearts, beating
around the bush: gossiping geese,
over-excited chickens at feeding time.

The eldest disembarks first at her steady pace,
still early as restaurant staff assemble.
She is calm, strong, orderly
as she patiently waits in quiet contentment.
Does the routine cutlery-clean
(just in case). A sunning tortoise
with hexagonal patterns on her frock.

Then comes the traveller, easily-bored,
frequent-flyer, cookie-bringer, bringing
stories and photos and new works of art
from dropped-off-picked-up-again hobbies.
She buzzes about the recent past, muses
over plans for the near future; a beehive of Busy.
Shares cookies, pours tea. More tea? More tea?

You know Sister Three has landed
as volumed voices start to chatter, arms
flailing like wings of a blue scrub-jay,
whose brain works over-overtime. Over-

enthusiastic, overwrought, over-worried.
Jet-lagged, energetic, she brings with her bags
of emotion. She leaves the bags aside.

The youngest one, cat-lady, shop-a-holic
bargain-hunter, carries shiny new things in her
claws. Late for obvious reasons. Smiles slyly,
haggles like a hyena, laughs the loudest,
unapologetic, unashamed. They laugh at her,
with her, grandma laughs too, mothers, daughters,
sisters; reinvigorated, reassembled, reunited.

Great-Aunt Rose

Your Great-Aunt Rose, they'd start –
and you'd wriggle away with a book –
was a remarkable woman.
You flipped a page and went on reading.

She had her own fleet of lorries –
what did lorries count for when you had
books and stories to explore? –
and she transported fish, said Dad,

*from Grimsby. And she had her own name
painted on the lorries*, Grandad added,
opening out his hands like a priest
distributing blessing.

You don't know where she took the fish;
you never asked. You do not know
who were the men who drove for her
or if she drove a lorry too?

Rose. Rose Archer. A name that makes
you think of her with bow and arrow
in her hand, shooting Pisces down
from night skies blue as sea.

KAYO CHINGONYI

Curfew

This was soldier curfew he says, apropos
of nothing, the way the best stories come
round this table that just about holds us,

bwali all but eaten, the flash of the thought
a flame lighting up his face. He rests the tip
of a finger in the space between his eyes,

past curfew there were no warning-shots.
Auntie chips in as if this were little more
than a scene they were rehearsing: *you had*

to have a man with you at all times, especially
at night, so my cousin would walk me home.
In trousers and squared shoulders she could pass.

She smiles a knowing smile at our scandalized
faces. Faces we've bent into anguished shapes
when she could smell a lie but let us improvise

wildly until, hoist by our respective petards,
we came clean, deferring to the knowledge
of a woman who was a girl who could climb

out of a window in hotpants and platforms,
dance to the last ache in her legs and make
it back before the cockerel crowed morning.

DAVID McKELVIE

A Half-Cut Sestina For My Long-Dead Devonshire Great-Aunt Eva Who Was No Great Drinker That I Know Of But Who Partook Of When Feeling Came

For she was reading Robert Graves –
the novelist, never poems –
and she was drinking damson wine.

Forever drinking damson wine
and singing Devon from the graves
in an overflow of poems.

For in all the world the poems
of all the Devon damson wine
in all the Devon damson graves…

>… Robert, Sir, remember her song
with its alcoholic gaze.

Betsey Trotwood sets the record straight

I wanted a niece not a nephew.
I make no bones about that. Swung my bonnet
at the idiot doctor when he told me.
Had to take the jewellers' cotton out of my ears –
I'd stuffed them to shut out the screams.
Silly girl was a baby herself. Left her to it,
just walked out and never came back.

Went home to chase donkeys off my grass
and look after Mr Dick. He was a baby too
with his giant kite. Still, after David turned up
ten years later like an urchin on my step
and called me *Aunt* I made up for it.
Oh Lord, I said, *what shall we do with him?*
and Mr Dick said *Give him a bath.*

ANGELA KIRBY

Aunt Amy's Parasol

For such a sombre woman it strikes an
unexpected note of frivolity, with those
flamboyant stripes of pink, white, yellow
and the oddly unexpected poker-work
handle, all strangely at odds with her,
the severe aunt we thought we knew,
in a no-nonsense maroon beret, jammed
on an uncompromising bob of grey hair,
her dingy tweeds, baggy cardigans, beige
lisle stockings and ancient brogues, but
now as we clear out her house, here she is
in a creased photograph, slim, smiling, her
hair languorously coiled beneath an outsize
ostrich-feathered hat set at a roguish angle,
wearing the long lace and fringed silk dress
which was then thought suitable for a day
at the Edwardian races, her parasol held
flirtatiously, leaning on the arm of some
tall young man who, it is almost certain,
will not be coming back from the Somme.

ISABEL S. MILES

Auntie Peg

She struggled with the wee bit garden after Jimmy died,
but kept it decent, like herself,
for widowhood was something ye maun thole.
Her life was punctuated by the weekly messages,
the news at six, the Sunday Post.
She liked a blether.

For casual visitors, like me, she had a tray with legs
that folded out to serve precarious treats,
a slice of new-baked rhubart tairt,
still warm, its golden sweetness melting
into sharp spring pink.

Behind well-polished glass the paper-thin
good cups, reserved for her at-homes,
looked down upon our ordinary feasts.

As Peg grew old, the shopping and the at-homes ceased.
She paid a man to cut the grass.
Once grown, her grandchild never reappeared –
but still, her younger sister, once a week,
her son, perhaps four times a year,
would visit.
And every day for thirty years my mum nipped up
to check she was all right.

Towards the end I think that she forgot
the mines were shut.
But still she hated Maggie Thatcher till the day she died.

Trapped by the stairs, she wouldn't shift
but sat and gazed to where kye graze
beside the Nith, eternally.
Or stared into the fire.
For when the council fitted other flats
with central heating,
she'd have none of it.
Coal did her fine.

It was a long wait, in death's waiting room.
Peg bore her boredom,
all her choices made.

Tailors

I had an aunt who lived in Englefield Green.
Her husband owned a small stuffed alligator.
I stayed with them while my mother had my sister.
My aunt gave me a plastic doll from a cracker.
Most days we made doll's clothes from felt.
We sewed poppers on, to fasten the parts together.

From time to time, I was allowed to examine the alligator.
It had rows of preserved teeth, like a sharp, bone zip.
My aunt had an electric sewing machine and could hem.
Sometimes, when I woke, there'd be a new doll's dress.
At others, we'd work together to produce two-part outfits.
When my parents returned, the doll had a full wardrobe.

The alligator still sat on my uncle's wooden desk.
Its small glass eyes reflected something close to envy.

JAN HERITAGE

Jon Snow and the Joyces

it starts with a slow plaiting of honeysuckle into
my then long hair *please hurry* I say to my mother
who hadn't been keen on a church do with all the
fuss and photographers who tend to take control
so my mother is lovingly plaiting honeysuckle into
my then long hair   I know that she isn't real or even
still alive   so this must be angel mother because
real mother didn't do that sort of thing beyond
the age of eight and certainly not at twenty five
when in fact   my hair was cut quite short   in a
bob   *please hurry* I say to angel mother who smiles
but has changed into the bridesmaid   the one who
married my then husband to be   much later   after
a long affair that predated the wedding I must now
hurry to get to   and I don't know this yet of course
but she helps me into my dress   although it isn't
my dress   not the one I bought in a vintage shop
in Islington   but some version of a meringue dress
with the top missing   so really   just a big petticoat
and a bra   people will laugh at me   but I must
leave   otherwise I will miss the bus   which stops
at the bottom of the hill at ten to the hour and
which is full of old ladies   all of whom seem to be
my Aunty Joyce   offering cardigans   *please hurry* I
say to the bus driver who reassuringly   is Jon Snow
and he accelerates so that all the Joyces laugh at
the thrill of it and ask to go faster and Jon becomes

---

one of those strong men on the Waltzer who are able to lean backwards and balance as the floor moves up and down and who spin the seats a lot or a little according to how pretty you are   and now the Joyces want to try their luck on the rifle range *please hurry* I say although I know that by now the guests at the church will be singing the second hymn and wondering why I am half naked on this of all days

JOAN MICHELSON

Aunt Syl

Aunt Syl threw her cane away and rocked
from hip to hip with every step she took.

A brave loner among married sisters,
she accepted loans of us on Sundays.

We'd be dressed in white embroidered frocks
with little trooping ducks across the breast,

white cuff socks and patent leather sandals
that fastened with a buckled strap and shone.

Her treat was one big balloon on a string
and one swan boat ride in the Public Gardens.

We have photos of these childhood outings.
Aunt Syl leans over us, a hand on each

of her darling sister-nieces. We smile.
It's not in the picture but I remember

when it was over and Aunt Syl gone,
we scrubbed her sticky kisses from our faces,

changed our clothes, and, giggling little curs,
outdid each other in our practised execution

of her rolling, raised-shoe walk.

KATE WHITE

She tells her nephew he's mad to get more tats

He's not her son so she can speak
her mind. They don't make him
more beautiful than he is already,
a shiny-eyed Jesus facing the light.
He displays his forearms
with palms up-cupped:
That one went a bit scabby –
when they did it again, the scar tissue hurt
he says, proudly. She tells him
about her old friend who got one done
in the 80s, *quite unusual then,*
and lived to regret it.
I'll never feel like that, he replies.
He hasn't yet had time to hate
a former self, or just drift off
from who he thought he was,
to see life fade in ways the eye
grows tired of. She's glad of that.

BRIAN DOCHERTY

My Favourite Aunt

(After Goya, *Doña Isabel de Porcel*, 1805)

My Aunt Isabel is formidable, do you not agree?
When I grow up, I want to be like her, emulate
her accomplishments. What a lot of big words
for a ten year old child, you are thinking, no?

If there is a more beautiful woman anywhere,
leaving aside our beloved royal family of course,
humour me. I may be precocious but I am still
part of this household; remember that, Señor.

When my Aunt came to stay with us last year,
she talked to me as if I were her own favoured
child, played cards with me, read to me from
Cervantes, talked to my parents about schooling.

Oh, you believe that girls should not be taught?
That you should be Master of your household
and estate, that women should play harpsichord
or dance for your entertainment, nothing more?

———

You will find that my Aunt has other ideas,
would not submit quietly to your authority
should you be foolish enough to declaim
This is how we do things in my house.

In any case, if you will take the word of this
small person, you would be better off looking
elsewhere; the word I overheard was *adventurer*;
my Aunt will find a better match than you.

MARGOT MYERS

The Sex Lives of Aunts

I

Auntie Rene
lived over the off-licence.

She was an usherette
in Streatham, and flighty

with customers. She'd get them
to take her home, ride pillion,

but my mother's grandmother
(Auntie Rene's mother, who plumped

up the cushions
everytime you moved)

would cast off
her corset at closing time

and leave it on the settee, like the shell
of an old lobster, so as to quell

any passion.

II

Auntie Lily played the piano in a pub and liked
Americans. But Uncle Mervyn, who was in the RAF

and became a gas engineer, carried her away
to Oswestry, where she played the piano in chapel

and wore his departed mother's hats. We found
a pile of Playboy magazines in the piano stool.

III

On my honeymoon
with your Auntie Agnes

    she gave us her bed and macaroni
cheese, took me for pastries

    in Princes Street, gave me her temperance
locket. I wore a purple skirt

    above the knee, she gave me a spurtle
to stir the porridge. She slept

    on the shelf in the kitchen alcove.
Sex seemed inappropriate.

Coal Tar

Still available. A throwback
to cigarette cards and iodine.
Victory Vs. Spit and polish.

The soap my aunt
scrubbed herself with
as if she were a stain.
Her water hard and scalding.

Used to ease her father's
signet ring from her finger
on hot, airtight days

and on me the time I slipped up.
I have never forgotten
the froth, the taste

or the way she set down
a tablet in the lodgers' bathroom
beside the copper taps,
like an unwritten house rule.

An orange threat.

CHARLOTTE EICHLER

Survivors

Our aunts drink tea for hours – they have no mirrors or clocks
but each other's faces tell the time. We wonder

why their hands shake and rattle the cups in their saucers.
We prowl the flat – the hallway dark with years of coats,

the dining room with carpets on the walls.
Each visit we think something will be different

but there's always the same red View-Master
with unchanging views of Prague, and no TV.

We draw elaborate tunnels and hold funerals for bees;
the cheese plant grows towards the window as if trying to escape.

Our aunts show us a glass case of curled-up figures
but all we want is the china cockatoo and toy koalas.

Their arms come towards us lined with numbers
and we wriggle away from their touch.

MATTHEW HAIGH

What Will Your Sims Do Now?

Like a good nephew, I save your computer
from the skip's slew of lifelong wreckage,
lug its black lake-weight back to my room
even though the tower is now a humming grave.
Inside still live the pixel kids
you abandoned to a timeless
paradise, still frolicking poolside,
spouting gibberish, clownish, in a summer
that will never end. They know nothing
of the absent god act you've pulled, these tiny
Adams and Eves in cherry-print kaftans.
I feed and clothe and shower them, these strange
skin cells you've shed in your swift exit,
my head haloed by the screen's heaven-
blue, the way yours must have been as you
crafted your craved reflection.
Here is the candy-haired
mohawk girl modelled on your ideal.
I push her around her little kitchen,
fingers lingering on the keys that yours
last touched. Her chip pan has caught fire.
The girl's face bursts open with tears.
Scorched walls. Her kitchen is
ruined. I can't console her.

Broken Biscuits

Aunt Hilda was a packer at the biscuit works,
sorting the custard creams and plain digestives,
bringing us bags of crumbed fragments
that tasted of each other, dipped in a hot brew.
The teapot was glazed with tannin inside
and out, its bitter tang offset with reject pink-
iced fancies. When Hilda cuddled me, I wriggled
free from the tight press of her arms and the need
I sensed at five or six but couldn't name. I told
my mother that I loathed the odour of vanilla.

Hilda was late-married to my uncle Fred, a nervy
mother's boy marched to the church door, we were
told, by brothers of the bride he never made
a wife. She wept daily at her sister's kitchen table;
broke open on the bus to Blackpool screaming
that God would make her pregnant with the child
she longed for. Sectioned to the Bedlam
we were all afraid of, bare rooms that stank of urine
and singed hair, Hilda, shocked into sanity but altered,
walked with us in the garden, quiet with blank eyes.

———

Fred was obsessed with cleanliness, feared
germs, contamination; wouldn't shake your hand.
And when he sickened like a child she fed him
with a spoon, nursed him, washed his clothes,
winding him into the sheet she hoped
would be his last. She found release among
the company of women on the packing line,
fattened on that sweet diet, smelling of chocolate
and vanilla, consuming the crumbs, never the whole thing.

Aunty

The cleaner eats her dinner against the tampon dispenser.
I can tell by the skin, the white meat of her bite, it's a Granny Smith.
She strips it to its spine, twists the stalk with her teeth,
tips brown beads into her palm, pockets them, bins the rest.
She catches me staring at her in the mirror,
'You thought I eat core like a savage?'
'No!' I pump soap, blast the dryer.
She kisses her teeth, laughs, *hmms* at the same time,
from the same mouth.
I thought only my Mum could do that.

Tannoy crackles, a god in the walls; there's a leak in the Men's.
She rises, sways, steadies herself on the sink.
I ask if she's ok. A pause.
A gap, generation wide, ocean-sized –
I should address a woman this age as Aunty.
Are you ok, Aunty? But we're not related.
She raises her eyebrows, closes her eyes, tries
to kiss her nose with her lips.
This means yes, weary *yes*.
It's the face my Mum makes to the offer of tea
when she comes home from her night shift.
Lurid green and white badges smiling for them,
Here to assist YOU! branded across their buckets, their breasts.
'Me, I'm OK O. Jus' a little back pain.'
In her Yoruba accent I hear, 'Jus' a little black pain.'

She stoops low for her bucket; I try to help her
but it's already scooped in deft hands,
hands I know if turned over
would have lifelines deep as knifewounds,
bistre as the vaccine scar on her fleshy arm.
She raises the bucket high, higher, grey water sloshing.
My eyes must widen, ready to bullfrog –
her laugh saves their amber rolling down my face, across the wet floor.
'Look at you, British girl.
You think we put any bucket on our head?'

I want to tell her *No! I know you don't*,
want to tell her a secret,
my Mum is Yoruba, or she was,
before she came to England.
But Aunty will ask, *What people? What town?*
I won't be able to answer.
A red sun will creep up my neck,
set on both sides of my face.
She'll be disappointed, know my ignorance,
my guilty sweep of a darker side under a carpet of Dad's white skin.

She resumes making a sea around my shoes,
leaves me an island. I stay silent,
watching her wet mop slap tiles
like an awkward tongue.

———————

Tannoy bellows louder this time.
'Moogee, we need you in the Men's NOW.'
I have a cousin called Moji,
I wonder if it meant to call the same name?
She told me it meant endless wealth,
whilst we sat at a bus stop sharing a box of chicken and chips.
Moji, she must be, grabs her mop and bucket,
mutters something to herself, or the god in the walls,
then stops at the door, calls over her shoulder:
'When you see your Mom, my sistah, greet har for me.
A fine, fine daughter with a head full of nothing.
Tell har to tek you to Nigeria. They will fill it for you good.'
My laugh echoes foreign against the lockers.

MIA

Elizabeth Garrett Anderson Wing

I am scared of my left breast
A tainted lineage
A blood line stained
by bad blood

To share so much in common despite
never having met
The psychic saw you standing at my shoulder
My left? I forget

But you had dyed your hair
from the raven black that hung to
below your belly

Concealing the threat
we pass from hand to hand
and chest to chest

For the Aunts of Eighties Metal

For those with spiked blonde hair
and those with brunette perms.
For those who pancaked their faces
and those who only kohled their eyes.
For those who wore Spandex on their thighs
and Lycra in their jumpsuits. For those
who wore tasselled cowboy chaps
and those who wore Stetsons and boots
and not a whole lot more. For youth gone wild
and hair gone up in flames. For pyrotechnics
and acrobatics across the stage.
For those who wore leather or pleather, studs or lace.
For those in hotel room bars
playing twelve-string guitars.
For them.

J V BIRCH

Auntie Australia

It's Sunday night, Skype time
and I feel the smile as my brother appears,
his son perched on his lap.

This is daddy's sister, your auntie in Australia.
And that's how it started – 'Auntie Australia' –
my nephew clapping and grinning.

I notice his lashes have grown,
his eyes are bluer, he's got a new tooth.
I attempt a screenshot – like netting a butterfly

as he plays with the keys,
sees himself in the corner of the screen,
beams and waves, looks back up at his dad.

We swap news of our fingertip family.
And after goodbyes, as their image disappears,
Charlie's grin is suspended, bridging

the distance, last to leave like the Wonderland cat's.

My oddest aunt

My Auntie Vi thought cabbages had souls,
that eating them was something of a sin;
Auntie Vi took hours to dry a single spoon,
being sunk in problematic thoughts again;
Auntie Vi had 'feet and bicycles';
she would cycle up from Exeter to London,
sleep in haystacks overnight –
she would never use a train or bus
and if you *mentioned* aeroplanes...!

Then she wrote the strangest book,
demanding science make a neutral sex
to bear the babies, satisfy
the sexual needs of men
so women could be free to have careers.
The Daily Mirror seized on it
(I think they might have laughed at it)
while Australian women queued
and fought for it.

Auntie Vi was suddenly wearing make-up,
furs, riding round in stylish cars;
eating cabbages without a second thought.

The book was called *Women in Bondage* (the 'bondage' being subservience) and it sold so well in Australia in the 1950s that Auntie Vi became rich. It was probably a forerunner of the modern feminist movement but never acknowledged as such, and is long out of print.

AMY EVANS

Sister

Womb   twinge   in   time
    colon   too, catching what pain-
               whispers
     of   muscle &   prox imity   a
       cross distance? neither know
        ledge nor phone call
             based

Second: womb   twinge   in   time
   not   telepathy   —   sororal
    and now you are in deed,
            two:
          sorosis

     a flesh   y   multiple
           fruit

   like   the   pine   apple
     or mul   berry
       derived

knowing ova ries of not one
    but   sever   al
        flow
        ers

these fruits too knew
  sister   ly
    contract
     -ion

    of
    the
daughter s, m
   other

KIM M. RUSSELL

Holiday in Clacton

When I was four,
my glamorous aunt
took me to Clacton
on a jaunt
with her boyfriend
and his boxer dog.
I was a pawn,
a red herring
at the seaside,
playing in the sand
while they held hands
and the bouncing,
drooling boxer
wriggled and weed
all over me.

My Colourful Aunt Rose

She didn't care
if colours clashed
or mismatched patterns
assaulted the eyes.

She had no time
for fashion fads
or following trends.

She wore what she liked,
said what she liked.

And we loved her for it.

How she would have loved today –
a hundred mourners
or more
lining the pews
in a hundred hues

with not one
hint of black.

The Alphabet Aunties

They flew across the Irish Sea each summer,
my Alphabet Aunties.
Wild swans with beehives.
Daughters of friends of friends, swooping
in broken arrow of womanhood,
migrating to the pulse of Ringo's tribal call.

Aisling the auburn, her insect-legged eyes
green as lime pickle
and twice as punchy.

Breda, gentle countrygirl,
clucking of lost stockings and cloakroom tickets.

Caoimhe, clicking kitten heels,
fag breath, raucous laughter.
Smelling of mints and the morning after.

Auntie D, Dymphne, whirling Diorissimo
with every flick of feathered scarf,
flying to catch up with sister

Eilish, whose energetic call of 'Let's go girls!'
long preceded Shania.

She gathered the flock for their descent
to the Cavern.
Lir's children: well off-course.

Grainne and Roisin,
fire and rose.
Shortest skirts, turquoise eyeshadow.
Homing in on Woolies for warpaint.
For sailors.

My unfurled mother, called briefly back
to nursing days, giggled away with her flock.

A small child crouches, entranced,
aware as a hare in a wheatfield,
ears pricked, absorbing
every zithering flash of glamour
from her stairy lair.

I can't remember when migration ceased.
A roost reclaimed
as father re-emerged from study, blinking.
My renewed mother
re-folding her apron-wings,
smoothing her transformation with a smile.

MARY ANNE CLARK

Familiar

My mum and her four sisters sound the same
when speaking on the phone, some strangers think.
As teenagers they used it for a game,
and tricked each other's boyfriends when they rang.
It's the consonants so sharp they make you blink;
it's the laugh that curved my embryonic ear,
the vowels that plucked my vocal cords' first twang.
And there, in the roots of each girl's voice, so clear,
that quavering voice that we no longer hear.

LILY BLACKSELL

From the Duck-Egg Blue Kitchen

David Beckham, gentleman that he is, stayed
stuck to the fridge long after you died.

'Step away from the cake' said the magnet
to his left, so I wondered when he last ate.

The rest of us still put mascara in stockings,
say 'sweetpea' and mean it, say mean things and sweat.

My cousin's email firmly told me to get
over one boy and under another. I don't

feel the need to do either or any one.
I ache like a woman; take away

the man, but know woe is not an option.
Someone please tell David he can sit down

now the ladies have left the room.
A wood pigeon's coo is how hard, so sad,

how hard, so sad. Meanwhile, Penny,
we miss you. This is just an echo of that.

GILL LEARNER

Auntie Bob's Feet

They've walked a world of lives from
baby lurches sailing home from Perth to straight-
laced pacing between bandaged men.

They pumped out hymns in a Nissen church,
moved on to heavy chords for villains, tender airs
for partings, hurry music for the chase.

They've felt the pillion rumble of an Ariel,
sweltered in rubber boots for victory,
double declutched a reluctant Morris Six.

In glossy black, they doorstepped promises
of smoother pavements, brighter streets,
then tattooed rage in council arguments.

They've stumbled at the crem for husband,
mother, only son, then returned to
forte-pianoing for arabesque and entrechat.

Last May they stomped in crimson straps
with nails of tangerine. Now, even trapped by
tautened sheets, they're beating time.

I sometimes hear her voice brekking

Fastening her headscarf, she's in two minds – wicker basket or tartan trolley: that 336 is a bugger for being cramped on pay day, and she only wants a few bits and pieces, the mekkings of a Dundee cake and some colouring books for her nieces.

    She takes a barley wine and a Babycham and crashes into family portraits and parties and louvre doors, like a Crimplene-coated wrecking ball. She lifts her skirt to shift her knickers, then cackles and says she's only checking.

    Bad language is sometimes *armholes* and *fecking*, she's not averse to the odd bit of necking, says *Eh up what you mekking? A fine mess?* Forever giving never tekking, I sometimes hear her voice brekking.

HILAIRE

On becoming an aunt

for Ana

Nothing changes in my body.
The clock
I've always lacked
still ticks not.
Nothing changes in my body,
but bit by bit something
like understanding grows,
and new love,
and budding wonder
at the tiny transformations
you effect in me.
I learn a new relation,
a dynamic
beyond conflict,
the fit of family
at last.

ROBERT HAMBERGER

Aunt Anna

We say her name. She high-heels through the room,
dripping with gold at her neck, lobes, wrists
and fingers, glittering the gloom.
Fishnets at fifty, she whistles a taxi, persists
in leopard spots, tiger stripes, black skirt slashed
to her thigh. That time some bastard
mugged her, she grabbed a cosh from her bag, bashed
his head till he scarpered. She'd get plastered
at our parties, sing *All I want is a table
and chair. I don't care, just a table and chair.*
She'd kick her leg high and never topple,
shimmying way past the midnight hour,
dabbing her ash, sloshing another swig,
cramming her minutes with life, making them big.

Acknowledgements

'Coal Tar', by Stephen Bone, was first published in *Smiths Knoll* 39 (2006).

'Curfew', by Kayo Chingonyi, first appeared in his pamphlet *The Color of James Brown's Scream* (Akashic, 2016).

'Survivors', by Charlotte Eichler, was previously published in the Flambard Poetry Prize *Prizewinners' Anthology* (2015) and on *And Other Poems* (2016).

'Sister', by Amy Evans, was first published in *VierSomes 001: Becky Cremin, Amy Evans, Frances Kruk, Nat Raha* (Veer Books, 2012) and celebrates the birth of her niece, Olivia Grace Wavell.

'Aunt Anna', by Robert Hamberger, was first published in *The North* 51 (2013).

'On becoming an aunt', by Hilaire, was first published in *Triptych Poets* 1 (Blemish Books, 2010).

'Aunt Amy's Parasol', by Angela Kirby, was first published in *The London Magazine* (2017).

'Aunty', by Rachel Long, was first published in *Homesickness and Exile* (Emma Press, 2014).

'The Butcher's Diamond', by Anita S. Pulier, was first published in her chapbook *The Lovely Mundane* (Finishing Line Press, 2013).

'Travelling with Isaac', by Anna Woodford, was first published in her collection *Birdhouse* (Salt, 2010).

About the poets

Natalya Anderson is a writer and former ballet dancer from Toronto, Canada. She won the Bridport Prize in 2014 for her poem 'Clear Recent History.' Her poems and feature writing have appeared in *Poetry London, Prac Crit, The Moth* and elsewhere.

J V Birch lives in Adelaide. Her poems have appeared in anthologies, journals and magazines across Australia, the UK, Canada and the US. She has two collections – *Smashed glass at midnight* and *What the water & moon gave me* – published by Ginninderra Press. She blogs at www.jvbirch.com

Lily Blacksell is a British writer living in New York, where she's working towards a poetry MFA at Columbia University. Her work has appeared in *Impakter, Poet's Country, Foothill* and *Magma*. She has written for *Boston Review, Sabotage* and *Prac Crit*. In 2016, Lily was nominated for a Pushcart Prize.

Stephen Bone's work has appeared in magazines and anthologies in the UK and the US. His first collection, *In The Cinema*, was published by Playdead Press in 2014. He has a pamphlet, *Plainsong*, due out with Indigo Dreams in 2017.

Carole Bromley lives in York. She has two collections with Smith/Doorstop: *A Guided Tour of the Ice House* and *The Stonegate Devil*, which won the 2016 York Culture Award. Her collection for children, *Blast Off!*, will be published in June 2017.

Kayo Chingonyi is a fellow of the Complete Works programme for diversity and quality in British poetry and the author of two pamphlets, *Some Bright Elegance* (Salt, 2012) and *The Color of James Brown's Scream* (Akashic, 2016). His first full-length collection, *Kumukanda*, is forthcoming from Chatto & Windus.

Mary Anne Clark studies English at Merton College, Oxford, where she won the 2016 Newdigate Prize. Her poems have appeared in *ASH, The Mays, The Kindling* and two Emma Press children's poetry anthologies.

Tracy Davidson writes poetry and flash fiction. Her work has appeared in various publications and anthologies, including *Mslexia, Modern Haiku, A Hundred Gourds, Journey to Crone, The Binnacle, The Great Gatsby Anthology* and *In Protest: 150 Poems for Human Rights.*

Brian Docherty lived in North London for many years before moving to East Sussex, where he is part of a growing community of writers, musicians and artists. His books include *Woke Up This Morning* (Smokestack Books, 2012) and *Independence Day* (Penniless Press, 2015).

Charlotte Eichler lives in West Yorkshire and works as an editor and medievalist. Her poems have appeared in magazines and anthologies including *Agenda, The Rialto* and *The Best New British and Irish Poets* (Eyewear, 2017). She was commended in the 2016 Battered Moons competition.

Amy Evans is the author of *The Report of the Iraq Enquiry: Poetic Summary* (ff press, 2017), the broadside *Stalking Gerard Manley Hopkins* (Salient Seedling/Woodland Pattern, 2016) and a third pamphlet *CONT.* (Shearsman, 2015). She performed her installation *SOUND((ING))S* at the ICA in 2016. She teaches at the University of Kent.

Matthew Haigh lives in Cardiff. His poems have appeared in a number of magazines and anthologies, including the children's poetry anthology *Falling Out of the Sky: Poems about*

Myths and Monsters (Emma Press, 2015). He has work forthcoming in *Aquanauts*, a Sidekick Books anthology of visual/concrete poetry inspired by water.

Robert Hamberger has been shortlisted for a Forward prize, awarded a Hawthornden Fellowship and featured as the *Guardian*'s Poem of the Week. He has published six pamphlets and three full-length collections, including *Torso* (Redbeck, 2007). He lives in Brighton.

Jan Heritage has had poems published in several magazines and publications, including *Magma, Brittle Star, Aesthetica* and three other Emma Press anthologies. She has completed the Royal Holloway MA in Creative Writing and currently lives and works in Brighton.

Hilaire was poet-in-residence at Thrive Battersea for Open Garden Squares Weekend 2016. Her poems and short stories have been published in several anthologies and various magazines, including *Brittle Star, Under the Radar* and *ARTEMISpoetry*. Her novel *Hearts on Ice* was published by Serpent's Tail in 2000.

Kathleen Jones' first collection, *Not Saying Goodbye at Gate 21*, won the Straid Award. Her recent pamphlet, *Mapping Emily*, won the 2016 Templar Iota Shots award. Her second collection, *The Rainmaker's Wife*, is due out with Indigo Dreams in 2017. Kathleen is a novelist and biographer and a Royal Literary Fund Fellow.

Angela Kirby was born in Lancashire but now lives in London, having spent a lot of time in France, Spain and the US. Her poems have won prizes and commendations in several major competitions. Shoestring Press published her last four collections and she is now working on her fifth.

Gill Learner grew up in Birmingham but now lives in Reading. She has won a number of prizes, including the Poetry Society's Hamish Canham Award, and been published in many magazines and anthologies. Her collections, *The Agister's Experiment* (2011) and *Chill Factor* (2016), are published by Two Rivers Press.

Rachel Long is a poet, curator and facilitator. She is an alumna of the Jerwood/Arvon Mentorship scheme and is currently assistant tutor to Jacob Sam-La Rose on the Barbican Young Poets programme. She is the leader of Octavia, a poetry collective for women of colour at Southbank Centre, London.

Gill McEvoy has had two collections published with Cinnamon Press and three pamphlets with HappenStance, the second of which, *The First Telling,* won the Michael Marks Award in 2015. She runs a poetry reading group, a Poetry Breakfast and a workshop group in her home town.

David McKelvie makes maps in Glasgow, lives in Greenock and writes mainly for himself aged twelve. His poems have appeared occasionally in a handful of publications.

Mia grew up in the hills and forests of mid Wales. Her poetry has appeared widely on postcards to friends, letters to lovers and on the backs of lavatory doors. She has previously been published in an anthology of poems when she was twelve years old.

Joan Michelson's recent publications include a second full collection, *Landing Stage* (Sentinel Books, 2017), which examines refugees and immigrants, and a chapbook, *Bloomvale Home* (Original Plus Books, 2016), which examines residents in a care home. 'Aunt Syl' is from *The Family Kitchen*, a work in progress.

Isabel S. Miles lives, writes and walks in the North Yorkshire Moors. She has published work in *WTD, The View from Here, Ink, Sweat and Tears, Shooter, Grey Sparrow Journal* and *Toasted Cheese*. One of her poems was shortlisted for the 2015 Keats-Shelley prize. She is currently working on a novel.

Winifred Mok is an actress and filmmaker (*Kin: Fallen Star*) with a passion for stories, books and site-specific theatre. She studied English Literature and Theatre Arts at the University of Birmingham. Her projects and poems explore the spaces of language, culture and identity.

Margot Myers, aunt and great-aunt, lives in Oxford. She has been placed or commended in several poetry competitions and shortlisted for the Bridport Flash Fiction prize. She has poems in *The Emma Press Anthology of Dance* (2015) and *Urban Myths and Legends* (Emma Press, 2016).

After retiring from her New York law practice, **Anita S. Pulier** served as a US representative for the Women's International League for Peace and Freedom at the United Nations. Her chapbooks *Perfect Diet, The Lovely Mundane* and *Sounds of Morning* are published by Finishing Line Press.

Kim M. Russell is a retired teacher. She has lived in North Norfolk for twenty-five years, where she is inspired by the coast, big skies, her cats and her wild garden. She writes poetry every day, from haiku and tanka to sonnets and villanelles.

Elisabeth Sennitt Clough lives in Norfolk with her husband and three children. Her pamphlet *Glass* was a winner in the inaugural Paper Swans pamphlet competition and has been shortlisted for Best Poetry Pamphlet in the 2017 Saboteur Awards. Her debut collection *Sightings* was published by Pindrop Press.

Ruthie Starling is a Shropshire-based poet and artist. She writes about nature, family and modern life. She has had work published in books and magazines and does regular readings. She is currently working on a novel, illustrating her children's book and preparing her first poetry collection.

As a child in Scunthorpe, **Rob Walton** had many lovely aunts. He now lives on Tyneside. He has been published by the Emma Press, Frances Lincoln, *Butcher's Dog*, IRON Press, Arachne and others. With sculptor Russ Coleman, he created the New Hartley Memorial Pathway and Concrete 64 for Fountain17. Oddness at www.linesofdesire.co.uk

Kate White lives in London and works part-time at the Poetry Society. Her pamphlet, *The Old Madness*, won the 2013 Poetry School/Pighog Press Pamphlet Prize and was a Poetry Book Society Pamphlet Choice.

Simon Williams was elected The Bard of Exeter in 2013 and founded the large-format magazine, *The Broadsheet*. Simon has seven published collections. His latest pamphlet, *Spotting Capybaras in the Work of Marc Chagall*, launched in April 2016 and his latest full collection, *Inti*, was published in July 2016.

Anna Woodford's poetry collection *Birdhouse* (Salt, 2010) won the Crashaw Prize. She is poet-in-residence at York University's CoMotion Centre and a Peer Reviewer for Creative Scotland. She has received a Leverhulme Award, a Gregory Award and has a doctorate in the poetry of Sharon Olds. www.annawoodford.co.uk

About the editors

Rachel Piercey is a poet and editor for adults and children. She regularly performs her poems and runs writing workshops at schools and festivals across the country. Rachel's poems have appeared in *The Rialto, Magma, Poems in Which, Butcher's Dog* and *The Poetry Review*, as well as various Emma Press pamphlets and anthologies, and in 2008 she won the Newdigate Prize. She lives in London.

Emma Wright worked in ebook production at Orion Publishing Group before leaving to found the Emma Press in 2012, with the support of the Prince's Trust Explore Enterprise programme. She lives in Birmingham.

The Emma Press

small press, big dreams

The Emma Press is an independent publisher dedicated to producing beautiful, thought-provoking books. It was founded in 2012 by Emma Wright in Winnersh, UK, and is now based in Birmingham. Having been shortlisted in both 2014 and 2015, the Emma Press won the Michael Marks Award for Poetry Pamphlet Publishers in 2016.

The Emma Press is passionate about making poetry welcoming and accessible. In 2015 they received a grant from Arts Council England to travel around the country with *Myths and Monsters*, a tour of poetry readings and workshops for children. They are often on the lookout for new writing and run regular calls for submissions to their themed poetry anthologies and poetry pamphlet series.

Sign up to the Emma Press newsletter to hear about their events, publications and upcoming calls for submissions. Their books are available to buy from the online shop, as well as in bookshops.

https://theemmapress.com
http://emmavalleypress.blogspot.co.uk

ALSO FROM THE EMMA PRESS

The Emma Press Anthology of the Sea
Edited by Eve Lacey
RRP £10 / ISBN 978-1-910139-45-5

In the *Anthology of the Sea*, poets ask how the human mind can fathom the ocean's depths. The sea emerges as at once strange and familiar, bearing witness to storms, ocean creatures and the human desire for freedom.

Dragonish, by Emma Simon
RRP £6.50 / ISBN 978-1-910139-64-6

Loss, love and various severed body parts are scattered throughout *Dragonish*. The poems are rooted in family, friends and home while also reaching into other worlds: the circus of possibilities, an earth-bound heavenly host, London's dryads and a nineteenth-century French brothel.

ALSO FROM THE EMMA PRESS

THE EMMA PRESS ANTHOLOGY OF MOTHERHOOD
Edited by Rachel Piercey and Emma Wright
RRP £10 / ISBN 978-0-9574596-7-0

An anthology which celebrates and examines the complexity of emotion surrounding motherhood. The darkest thoughts of exhausted mothers are sensitively portrayed, as poets expose the weight of responsibility behind the state of motherhood, and question the expectations society places on mothers.

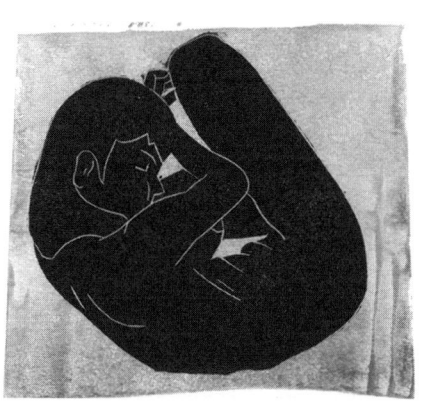

IF I LAY ON MY BACK I SAW NOTHING BUT NAKED WOMEN
By Jacqueline Saphra, with colour illustrations by Mark Webber
RRP £12.50 / ISBN 978-1-910139-06-6

A sumptuous sequence of prose poems about the eccentric activities of parents and step-parents, as seen from a child's perspective. The poems are illustrated with linocuts which celebrate real bodies and complement the vivid atmosphere.

ALSO FROM THE EMMA PRESS

The Emma Press Anthology of Age
Edited by Sarah Hesketh
RRP £10 / ISBN 978-1-910139-31-8

The Emma Press Anthology of Age is a collection of poems which challenge, celebrate and give age a voice, finding humour amidst heartbreak and comfort within pain.

Goose Fair Night, by Kathy Pimlott
With an introduction by Clare Pollard
RRP £6.50 / ISBN 978-1-910139-35-6

A generous, jellied feast of a book, full of sharp-eyed yet tender details about friendship, family and familiarity. Pimlott ranges around the country to offer her warmly incisive take on living and loving in a gorgeous, unstable world.

ALSO FROM THE EMMA PRESS

HOMESICKNESS AND EXILE
POEMS ABOUT LONGING AND BELONGING
Edited by Rachel Piercey and Emma Wright
RRP £10 / ISBN 978-1-910139-02-8

How does it feel to be a foreigner? Can you choose where you call home? *Homesickness and Exile* is a collection of poems about the fundamental human need to belong to a place.

MALKIN, by Camille Ralphs
RRP £5 / ISBN 978-1-910139-30-1

Malkin brims and bubbles with the voices of those accused in the Pendle Witch Trials of 1612. Thirteen men and women – speaking across the centuries via Ralphs' heady use of free spelling – plead, boast and confess, immersing the reader in this charged and dangerous time in history.

ALSO FROM THE EMMA PRESS

Slow Things: Poems about Slow Things

Edited by Rachel Piercey and Emma Wright
RRP £10 / ISBN 978-1-910139-16-5

Slow walks, slow thoughts and slow afternoons in the sun provide inspiration for the poets in *Slow Things*, an anthology which celebrates taking life at a leisurely pace and existing in the present.

AWOL

By John Fuller and Andrew Wynn Owen,
with colour illustrations by Emma Wright
RRP £12.50 / ISBN 978-1-910139-28-8

In rural Wales, John Fuller has composed a letter on the subject of travel: warning against it, and wondering about people's presences and absences. Andrew Wynn Owen replies with enthusiasm, matching John's poetic form while hopping from gallery to garret.

ALSO FROM THE EMMA PRESS

Mildly Erotic Verse
Edited by Rachel Piercey and Emma Wright
RRP £10 / ISBN 978-1-910139-34-9

Mildly Erotic Verse skips the mechanics and dives straight into the emotional core of sex, celebrating the diversity and eccentricity of human sexuality.

DISSOLVE to: L.A., by James Trevelyan
RRP £5 / ISBN 978-1-910139-37-0

What does it mean to die in a movie scene? To exist on the peripheries? Trevelyan takes twelve cult action films of the 1980s and 90s and gives life where it was extinguished too early.

ALSO FROM THE EMMA PRESS

True Tales of the Countryside, by Deborah Alma
With an introduction by Helen Ivory
RRP £6.50 / ISBN 978-1-910139-26-4

Deborah Alma's poems are gloriously pungent, teeming with colours, textures and smells. Eyeballs pop, fresh piss steams and women come – loudly – in poems which often startle with their honesty and intimacy.

The Held and the Lost, by Kristen Roberts
RRP £5 / ISBN 978-0-9574596-8-7

A moving collection of distinctly Australian poems about love, marriage and family life. Roberts is laid-back but precise as she sketches out sympathetic portraits of characters and relationships against the backdrop of swaying eucalypts, roses and occasional rain.

Urban Myths and Legends
Poems about Transformations
Edited by Rachel Piercey and Emma Wright
RRP £10 / ISBN 978-1-910139-24-0

A lively collection of poems by modern poets who have taken inspiration from the Roman poet Ovid's *Metamorphoses*. The poems all tell stories which include a transformation – some inspired directly by the *Metamorphoses* and some completely new and of our time. Wings sprout, leaves fall and no state is certain, as the poets channel Ovid's mischief and whisper tales of just and unjust deserts.